CW00502742

Date	Name	Form
November	Gina Bartlett	U3H
Nov 28/61	AnnChih	U3S

If found please return this book to
Headington School, Oxford

HEINEMANN
PLAYS

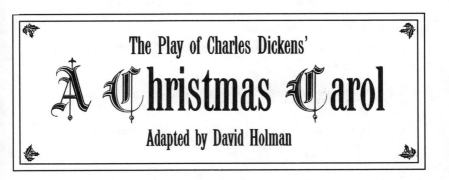

The Play of Charles Dickens'

A Christmas Carol

Adapted by David Holman

Introduction and questions by Lawrence Till

Series editor: Lawrence Till

Heinemann

Heinemann Educational,
a division of Heinemann Publishers (Oxford) Ltd
Halley Court, Jordan Hill, Oxford OX2 8EJ
OXFORD   LONDON   EDINBURGH
MADRID   ATHENS   BOLOGNA   PARIS
MELBOURNE   SYDNEY   AUCKLAND   SINGAPORE   TOKYO
IBADAN   NAIROBI   HARARE   GABORONE   PORTSMOUTH NH (USA)

First published in the *Heinemann Plays* series 1994
94 95 96 97 10 9 8 7 6 5 4 3 2

A catalogue record for this book is available from the British Library on request.
ISBN 0 435 23305 X

Caution
This play is fully protected by copyright. Any enquiries concerning the rights for
professional or amateur stage production should be addressed to David Holman,
48 Castlewood Rd, London N16 6DW

Cover design by Keith Pointing

Original design by Jeffery White Creative Associates

Typeset by CentraCet Limited, Cambridge

Printed by Clays Ltd, St Ives plc

Acknowledgements
The author would like to thank the musical director, Andy Dodge, for the selection and
arrangement of the carols.

CONTENTS

INTRODUCTION

Charles Dickens' life

Charles Dickens was born in Portsmouth in 1812. His father was a clerk in the Navy pay office. In Portsmouth, Dickens attended a small, inexpensive school run by a young teacher.

When Dickens was eleven his family moved to London. His father wasn't earning much money and when Dickens was twelve, his family found him a job in the Warren's blacking factory. He hated the job and found the experience very humiliating.

Shortly after Dickens started work his father was imprisoned for debt in the Marshalsea prison. Dickens' mother and their other five children also went to live in the prison. Charles visited his family regularly in prison and the experience of poverty and misery was to remain with him as a bitter memory throughout his life.

Dickens continued his education at the Wellington House Academy where he remained until the spring of 1827. He then worked as an office boy, studied shorthand and became a reporter in the House of Commons for the *Morning Chronicle*. During the 1830s he also wrote sketches for a number of journals.

In 1836 when he was 25, Dickens published the first part in a serialisation called *The Pickwick Papers*. The serialisation was very popular and financially very successful.

Dickens the writer

By the time he wrote *A Christmas Carol*, Dickens was a very popular writer. He wrote many stories which were serialised in monthly magazines. Sales of magazines went up when one of Dickens' stories was included and people waited eagerly for each

instalment. The Victorian public liked his larger-than-life characters, the comic parts of his stories, the mysteries he created and
the sentimental parts of his stories.

However, Dickens did not write stories just to entertain his
audience. He was aware of the problems and injustices in society
and he used his novels to make people think about other people's
struggles. His novels include subjects such as poverty, bad
working conditions, especially for children, and poor housing and
health conditions. He also wanted to make people think about
their own personal lives so his novels have a strong moral
message.

Dickens understood that people are more likely to take notice of
serious issues when they feel involved with the characters in a
story than if you preach at them. His novels are a clever combi-
nation of elements to make you laugh or cry and elements to make
you think seriously.

A Christmas Carol

Dickens wrote *A Christmas Carol* in 1843 to make people aware of
the terrible plight of the children of the poor. It was published on
17 December 1843 and by 24 December it had sold 6,000 copies.
Dickens called it 'a most prodigious success – the greatest, I think,
that I have ever achieved.'

In 1843, Dickens visited the Field Lane Ragged School and was
appalled by what he saw there. Ragged Schools catered for the
very poorest, hungry children who roamed the streets. The schools
tried to teach these children the basics of reading and writing.
Dickens first thought of writing a pamphlet called 'An Appeal to
the People of England on behalf of the Poor Man's Child'. However,
he realised that far more people would take notice of the conditions of the poor if he wrote about them in a story. The thought
that Tiny Tim might die would have tugged at the heartstrings of

his Victorian audience and would have encouraged them to think about the needs of children in poverty everywhere.

Through the story of the tight-fisted miser, Scrooge, Dickens gave his readers a strong moral message about the dangers of wanting money for its own sake compared with the joys of sharing your life and possessions with other people.

A Christmas Carol is still widely read today and appears in many versions including illustrated re-tellings of the story for young children. Hardly a Christmas goes by without a version of *A Christmas Carol* appearing on television in one form or another.

A Christmas Carol: the play by David Holman

During his lifetime, Charles Dickens' novels were regularly adapted for the stage. The nineteenth-century adaptors didn't ask his permission – they just bought a copy of the book and, very quickly and often carelessly, turned the novel into a stage play. They would turn an eight hundred page book into a play lasting perhaps a couple of hours. In all cases these stage versions were a pale shadow of the original novel. But, one must admit, these stage plays were very popular in the theatre of the day, largely because Dickens himself was so popular. The audiences considered even cut-up Dickens better than most other plays being presented at the time.

A Christmas Carol is different because it is a short story. You can tell the story in the theatre in an hour and half because that is roughly the time it would take to read it out loud. You don't have to cut away large parts of his story. Dickens is a very dramatic writer, much of the story is told in speech, and therefore it is not very difficult to change this story into a stage play. Almost all of what you will read here is in Dickens' own words. I wouldn't attempt to improve on them. However, sometimes Dickens indicates a situation that he doesn't want to describe in full, for example the Christmas party in Fred's house. But even here he gives you so much detail that no great skill is needed to create a lively scene. I have added a few touches of my own when I felt they were needed and were in the spirit of the original.

What a writer adapting this story has to do though, is cut. When you read a story you generally read faster than the words can be spoken out loud. Speeches or scenes which you are quite happy to read to yourself can appear too long when spoken on the stage. So I have slightly shortened the action of Dickens' story but, I hope, always in the spirit of this great writer. I first came to know this story in a film version when I was very small. I have loved it ever since and hope you will enjoy it too.

About the Author

David Holman has written more than 70 works for stage, radio, film and opera which have been performed for or by children. His work has been translated into many languages and has been produced on every continent.

Many of these works have explored environmental questions. These include his most performed play *Drink The Mercury* (1972) about the effects of heavy metal pollution on the fisherman of Minamata in Japan; *Adventure in the Deep* (1973) whose subject is the despoliation of the oceans; *Big Cat, Bad Coat* (1980) and *Solomon's Cat* (1987) both concerned with endangered species in Africa; and *Operation Holy Mountain* (1989) on the second coming of the patron Saint of animals, Francis of Assisi.

More recently David Holman has produced a stage adaptation of a story by Nikolai Gogol called *Diary of a Madman* which toured the Soviet Union in 1991 after winning the Sydney Critics Prize. Further stage adaptations include *Billy Budd* (1991) and *Beauty and the Beast* (1992). He has also written a film script, *No Worries*, filmed in Australia.

Other widely performed plays are *No Pasaran* (1976), *The Disappeared* (1979), *Peacemaker* (1980), *No Worries* (1984) and *The Small Poppies* (1986).

A Christmas Carol

Charles Dickens

List of Characters

Narrators
Ebenezer Scrooge
Fred Scrooge *His nephew*
Mrs Fred Scrooge
May Scrooge *Scrooge's sister*
Ebenezer Scrooge *Aged eight*
Ebenezer Scrooge *Aged 18 and
    then 20*
Bob Cratchit
Mrs Cratchit *His wife*
Martha Cratchit *His daughter*
Belinda Cratchit *His daughter*
Tiny Tim Cratchit *His young
    son*
The Ghost of Jacob
    Marley *Scrooge's partner*
The Ghost of Christmas Past
The Ghost of Christmas Present
The Ghost of Christmas Future
First Philanthropist
Second Philanthropist
Mr Fezziwig
Mrs Fezziwig
Dick Wilkins *An apprentice*

Elsie from the warehouse
Belle *Young Scrooge's beloved*
Charlie *Belle's husband*
Little Charlie *Their son*
A musician at the Fezziwig
    warehouse
Tupper *A friend of Fred*
Florence *Tupper's beloved*
A party guest
Another party guest
Another party guest
The child Ignorance
The child Need
First Stockbroker
Second Stockbroker
Third Stockbroker
Mrs Maggs *Scrooge's cleaning
    woman*
Mrs Delaney *A rag and bone
    collector*
A pallbearer
A second pallbearer
A boy in the street

ACT ONE

Scene One

The house lights go down.

Singing voices are heard as the Carollers enter the stage area. From the first line sung by a single voice, the wassail builds until all of the assembled group of Carollers are singing.

Caroller   Here we come, we come.

Carollers   A Happy New Year, we come, we come.

Carollers   Here we come. We come.

Carollers   A Happy New Year, we come, we come.

Carollers   Here we come, we come.

Carollers   A Happy New Year, we come, we come.

Carollers   Here we come, we come.

Carollers   Here we come a wassailing,
Among the leaves so green.
Here we come a wandering,
So fair to be seen.
Love and joy come to you,
And to you our wassail too.
And God bless you and send you,
A Happy New Year.

Male Carollers   We have got a little purse,
Of stretchy leather skin.
We want a little of your money,
To line it well within.
Love and joy come to you,
And to you our wassail too.
And God bless you and send you,

A Happy New Year.

Children Carollers   Good master and good mistress,
While you're sitting by the fire,
Pray think of us poor children,
Who are wandering in the mire.
Love and joy come to you,
And to you our wassail too.
And God bless you and send you
A Happy New Year.

Narrator   Ladies and gentlemen. And especially to all my young friends, good evening. May I present our Company of Poor Carollers who, tonight, with your permission, will present a ghost story. A ghost story of Christmas.

Narrator   And so a little Christmas Ghost music, if you please.

Sung in ghostly voices.

Carollers   Here we come a wassailing,
Among the leaves so greeeeeeeeeen.

Narrator
(Optional section)   Ladies and gentlemen, excuse me. A word in the ears of the youngsters only. You shavers, the Company, as you will observe, is so many.

He indicates this with his hands.

But the number of persons and the number of ghosts we must present in this story is so many.

He widens his hands.

Therefore, my young friends, if one appears before you calling himself Fred and then, some little while later, enters in a new coat and hat and perhaps a new moustache and is then addresssed as Tom, then you will know the reason – that we cannot afford to provide you with a new Tom and must give you an old Fred disguised.

Narrator	And now my young hearts come back with us in your imagination to the night of Christmas Eve. Over one hundred years ago.
Carollers	God Bless you Merry Gentlemen,

Carollers God Bless you Merry Gentlemen,
Let nothing you dismay.
For Jesus Christ our Saviour,
Was born on Christmas Day.
To save us all from Satan's power,
When we have gone astray.
Oh tidings of comfort and joy, comfort and joy,
Oh tidings of comfort and joy.

They continue to hum through the following speech.

Narrator Come with me down ice-covered streets, lit only with gas lamps, to a certain miserable street and a certain gloomy house in the heart of London town. Miserable and cold is the weather. But not so bleak, not so miserable and not so cold as the man who sits within. Ebenezer Scrooge of the firm of Scrooge and Marley, dealers in money.

Ebenezer Scrooge (this actor has been the only one not part of the Carolling group) and Bob Cratchit are seated at their desks. Bob Cratchit is listening to the carol outside and is enjoying it. Scrooge hits his clerk for doing do.

Scrooge Damn blast that noise! Cease your squawking!

The carol stops.

Can't a man be busy with his accounts without suffering this infernal din?

Cratchit It is Christmas Eve, Sir.

Scrooge Christmas Eve! Pah! The end of the year accounts must be settled, Christmas Eve or no, Cratchit. If a man owes me money he'll settle his account on Christmas Eve as well as any day.

Cratchit   Yes, Mr Scrooge.

The clock strikes five o'clock. The Carollers softly sing.

Carollers   In the bleak mid winter, frosty wind made moan,
Earth stood hard as iron, water like a stone.
Snow had fallen, snow on snow, snow on snow,
In the bleak mid winter, long ago.

They continue humming.

Cratchit   Mr Scrooge?

Scrooge   No.

Cratchit   I was just going to observe that it was five o'clock, Mr Scrooge.

Scrooge   And your time is seven o'clock. Which means, if you will allow me to observe it, that you are still two hours in my debt for the day's work.

Cratchit   Might I be allowed, just the once, Sir, to slip out to the toyshop which closes at, I believe, six, Sir? I saw something cheap and bright in the window for my boy Tim.

Scrooge   Toyshop? Bah! Hang your Tim, Sir, for all I care. Seven o'clock is your time and not a second sooner.

Cratchit   Yes, Mr Scrooge.

Scrooge   Christmas Eve! Bah! World's gone mad. Your pen, Sir! If you please.

Scrooge indicates that Cratchit should start his accounting work again immediately. Cratchit starts to write. The Narrator, who has been watching all this, continues.

Narrator   'Scrooge and Marley' said the sign above the door.

But Marley was dead. Scrooge never painted out his partner's name so sometimes people new to the business called Scrooge, 'Scrooge' and sometimes 'Marley' but he answered to both names. It was all the same to him. Marley was dead. Had died seven years ago this very night. For seven years Scrooge had not spent more than one moment's thought on his dead partner but tonight . . . tonight my young shavers . . . he will have reason to think much about Jacob Marley.

Scrooge has been looking elsewhere and turns to find Cratchit attempting to warm his hands at the solitary candle. Scrooge immediately removes Cratchit's candle to his own side of the desk.

Oh he was a tight-fisted hand at the grindstone, Scrooge. A squeezing, rasping, scraping old sinner. Hard and sharp as flint from which no steel ever struck warming fire. No spring sun could warm, no wintry weather chill him.

The church clock strikes six. The humming of the carol stops. Cratchit appeals voicelessly to Scrooge to let him go. Scrooge indicates 'no' emphatically. Cratchit resignedly gets back to his copying. He is very cold.

Narrator   No one every stopped Scrooge in the street with a 'My dear Scrooge, how are you? Will you come and see me?'

Narrator   No beggar asked him for a ha'penny, no children asked him the time of day, no lost traveller would ask directions of him.

Narrator   Even the blindman's dog knew him, hurrying his sightless master into a doorway to avoid him.

Narrator   But all this satisfied Scrooge, for now he could be alone with himself and his money.

We hear the sound of Scrooge's nephew, Fred. He is heard laughing. Fred Scrooge enters, possibly through the audience, with his wife.

Narrator Of all the world only one person still worked for Scrooge's salvation – his nephew Fred.

Mrs Fred Fred! Fred Scrooge!

Fred My dear, it won't take a moment.

Mrs Fred But why?

Fred Because he is my uncle. He will be invited by no one else to Christmas dinner so we must invite him.

Mrs Fred Good if he would come. But he won't come.

Fred Probably not.

Mrs Fred He's never come.

Fred True. My dear, it's Christmas. Give me a kiss.

Mrs Fred Close your eyes.

Fred Scrooge does so.

Fred Closed, my dear.

Mrs Fred Scrooge is making a snowball.

Mrs Fred Tight?

Puckering his lips ready for a kiss.

Fred Yes.

And Mrs Scrooge stuffs the snowball right down his neck. She runs off laughing. Fred Scrooge laughs as he wipes the snow from his collar. Then he knocks at the door of Ebenezer Scrooge's office. There is a grunt from within. Fred enters.

A Merry Christmas, Uncle. God save you!

Scrooge Bah! Humbug!

Fred   Christmas a humbug, Uncle? You don't mean that, I'm sure.

Scrooge   I do. Merry Christmas? What reason do you have to be merry? You're poor enough.

Fred   And what reason do you have to be miserable? You're rich enough.

Scrooge   Bah! Humbug!

Fred   Don't be cross, Uncle.

Scrooge   What else can I be when I live in such a world of fools as this? What's Christmas for you but a time for finding yourself a year older and not an hour richer?

Fred   Uncle!

Scrooge   Uncle. Uncle! Nephew! You keep Christmas in your own way and let me keep it mine.

Fred   Keep it? But you don't keep it.

Scrooge   Let me leave it alone then! Much good may it do you.

Fred   Surely, Uncle, a thing can do us good without us making money from it. And so I say – Bless Christmas.

Bob Cratchit applauds this thought. Then he sees Scrooge glaring at him and his applause changes to a rubbing of his hands. He then starts to swing his arms as if to keep warm, still looking at Scrooge.

Scrooge   Another sound from you, Sir, and you will keep Christmas by losing your situation!

Fred   Don't be angry with your clerk, Uncle. Come, dine with us tomorrow.

Scrooge   I'd sooner starve.

Fred   But why? Why?

Scrooge	Why did you get married after I forbad it?
Fred	Because I fell in love.
Scrooge	Because you fell in love. Good afternoon.
Fred	I'm sorry with all my heart to find you so resolute but our invitation is here.

Placing printed invitation on Scrooge's desk.

	And you shall have it. We will lay a place for you as we do every year.
Scrooge	Don't trouble yourself. Good afternoon.
Fred	Merry Christmas.
Scrooge	Good afternoon.
Fred	And a happy New Year.
Scrooge	Good afternoon!

Giving Bob a small coin.

Fred	A merry Christmas to you, Bob Cratchit, and to your family.
Cratchit	The same to you, Sir. The compliments of the season.
Scrooge	Good afternoon!
Fred	Merry Christmas to all.

As Fred leaves.

Cratchit	Indeed so.

Scrooge is about to speak.

Carollers	Deck the halls with bails of holly, Falalalala falalala. 'Tis the season to be jolly, Falalalala falalala. Fill the reed cup, drain the barrel, Falalalalal falalala.

Troll the ancient Christmas Carol.
Falalalala falalala.

Scrooge looks around for something to throw as he speaks. He screws up Fred's invitation into a missile.

Scrooge You keep wife and family on fifteen shillings a week and you talk of Merry Christmas. Madman!

Cratchit But Mr Scrooge!

Scrooge goes to the door ready to assault the Carollers.

Scrooge Surrounded by lunatics and squawkers.

The carol stops. The Carollers move and take up position outside his door. One looks through the keyhole. (This does not imply that there should be a real door.)

Carollers See the flowing bowl before us,
Falalalala, falalala.

Scrooge tiptoes towards the door, missile raised.

Caroller Shh.

Scrooge stops and goes back into the room. The Caroller looks through the keyhole again and conducts.

Carollers Strike the harp and join the chorus,
Falalalala falalala.

Scrooge has returned, missile raised.

Caroller Shsh.

Scrooge stops and walks back towards his desk.

Carollers Follow me in merry measure,
Falalalala, falalala.

Scrooge has come forward again.

Caroller Shh.

Scrooge now stays where he is. The Caroller looks through the keyhole.

Singing very fast.

Carollers   Whilst we sing of beauty's treasure,
Falalalala, falalala.

And the Carollers, knowing what is coming, rush off. Scrooge lets out a cracked roar and rushes out. The Carollers have retreated and disappeared. Scrooge now faces, with his arm and missile raised, two lady philanthropists. The second of these carries a ledger. Scrooge, embarrassed by his possession of the missile, lowers it.

First Philanthropist   The firm of Scrooge and Marley, I believe. Have we the pleasure of addressing Mr Scrooge or Mr Marley?

Second Philanthropist   Marley?

Scrooge   My partner, Jacob Marley, has been dead these seven years. He died seven years ago this very night.

She shows Scrooge her charitable credentials.

First Philanthropist   We have no doubt his generosity is well represented by his surviving partner.

Second Philanthropist   Partner.

Scrooge   Generosity you say?

First Philanthropist   Yes, Mr Scrooge. At this festive season of the year, it is more than usually desirable that we should provide for the poor who suffer greatly in this cold season. Hundreds of thousands are in the greatest need in this city.

Scrooge   Are there no prisons?

First Philanthropist   Plenty of prisons, alas.

Second Philanthropist   Alas.

Scrooge   And the workhouses, are they still in operation?

First Philanthropist   But my dear Sir, these hard institutions offer no comfort to the poor at this festive season and so a few of us are attempting to raise a fund to buy the poor some food and drink and means of warmth. What can I put you down for?

Scrooge   Nothing.

First Philanthropist   You wish to be anonymous?

Second Philanthropist   Anonymous?

Scrooge   I wish to be left alone. I don't make merry myself at Christmas and I can't afford to make idle people merry. Through taxation I help pay for the prisons and the workhouses and that costs me enough. Those that are badly off must go there.

First Philanthropist   Many cannot go there and many would rather die.

Second Philanthropist   Rather die.

Scrooge   And if they would rather die they had better do it and decrease the surplus population. Besides, excuse me, I don't know that.

First Philanthropist   If you would come with us through the streets we have walked down tonight and see the poor and see the destitute, see through their eyes the passers-by laden down with Christmas riches, you would know it then, Sir. You would know it then.

Second Philanthropist   Know it then.

Scrooge   It's not my business. It is enough for a man to understand his own business and not to interfere with other people's. Good afternoon ladies.

Seeing it is useless to take the matter further, the ladies begin to make their disappointed exit. Scrooge has turned his back on them. Cratchit has

*got up and, taking the small coin that Fred Scrooge
has given him from his pocket, he modestly slips it
to them before they leave. They take it gratefully
and depart.*

None of my business. None of my business.

*The clock strikes seven. Cratchit indicates that his
day's work is done and starts to clear his desk.*

You'll want all day tomorrow, I suppose?

Cratchit   If quite convenient, Sir.

Scrooge   It's not convenient and it's not fair. If I were to stop
you a half-a-crown for it you'd think yourself ill-
used I'll be bound.

No reaction from Cratchit.

And yet you don't think me ill-used when I pay a
day's wages for no work?

Cratchit   It is only once a year, Sir.

Scrooge   A poor excuse for robbing a man's pocket every
twenty-fifth of December. But I suppose you must
have the whole day. Be here all the earlier the next
morning.

Cratchit   Yes, Mr Scrooge.

Cratchit takes his fifteen shillings from the desk.

Thank you, Mr Scrooge.

*Cratchit exits from the office. Carollers sing as
Scrooge clears his desk. As Scrooge does this,
Cratchit snatches up some snow and makes a
snowball which he whirls at the office. Inside,
Scrooge is putting on his coat and hat ready to go
out. Cratchit tries to slide on the icy street and exits
humming.*

Scene Two

Carollers   Now to the Lord sing praises,
All you within this place,
Like we true loving brother,
Each other to embrace.
For the merry time of Christmas.
Is drawing on apace,
And it's tidings of comfort and joy,
Comfort and joy,
Oh tidings of comfort and joy.

Narrator   Jacob Marley was dead. Imagine then the emotions of Ebenezer Scrooge when, after he had taken his melancholy supper at his usual melancholy tavern and after he had read all the free newspapers in that tavern and passed what remained of the evening in studying in his bank book what people still owed him money, imagine his emotions when, standing at the door of his melancholy house, the door knocker which he had seen night and morning for many years had now not the appearance of a door knocker at all – but that of Jacob Marley's face!

Scrooge, during this narration, has passed across the stage from the office to the front door (without doing any of the actions described).

Scrooge   Aghhhhhhhhhhh.

Narrator   And not a dead face neither.

Scrooge   Aghhhhhhhhhhhh.

Narrator   Then all at once it was a door knocker again.

There is a pause.

Scrooge   Agh. Hmm. Humbug! Something I ate playing tricks on me. That cheese didn't agree with me.

Narrator	Marley's face or a piece of undigested cheese playing tricks on Scrooge's eyes? He was startled. Even more startled when, climbing the stairs of his dark abode, what was that cascading down the wide dark stairway towards him but, drawn by a dozen ghostly nags and driven by a skeleton in undertaker's clothes – A HEARSE!?

Through this, the music is combined with sound effects to amplify Scrooge's vision. This mixes with Scrooge's screams as he stops on the stairs.

Scrooge	Nooooooooooooooooooooooo.

The noise dies away and with it the music. Scrooge looks around. He speaks in a feeble voice.

Humbug.

Scrooge starts to get into his night clothes. He is scared. There is a tremendous clanging of distorted bells which deafens Scrooge.

Ghostly Voice

Scroooooooooooooooooooogggggggggggeeeeeeeeeeeeeee.

He falls to his knees, holding his ears.

Spoken even more feebly.

Scrooge	Humbug!

We hear the sound of doors opening and slamming, cries and groans, rattle of chains.

Humbug still. I won't believe it.

There is silence. Then, a chord of music and a far-off voice.

Speaking from off the stage.

Jacob	Scrooge. Ebenezer Scrooge!
Scrooge	Jacob? No. No. No. Go away. I don't believe it. I won't believe it.

From off the stage.

Jacob   Scrooge.

Scrooge   Oh God, save me.

We hear the crashing sound of a door opening. Scrooge is head in hands and does not see the ghost of Jacob Marley has entered behind him.

It's not. It's not. It's not.

Scrooge looks round and sees Jacob Marley.

It is! Jacob!

Marley stands there. He is bound with a great chain, with cash boxes and bank books attached.

Who are you?

Jacob   In life, I was your partner Jacob Marley. You don't believe in me.

Scrooge   I don't.

Jacob   Why do you doubt your senses, Scrooge?

Scrooge   Humbug. I'm dreaming you. You don't exist. It was that morsel of cheese I gobbled. You're just a figment of the cheese! Humbug.

We hear a great mournful groan from Jacob Marley.

Agh. Mercy!

Jacob   Do you believe in me or not?

Scrooge   I do. I must. But why do spirits walk on earth and why do they come to me?

Jacob   It is required of every man that the spirit within him should walk abroad among his fellow men. And if that spirit goes not forth in life, it is condemned to do so after death. Ohh.

Scrooge   You are chained. Tell me why.

Jacob   I wear the chain I forged in life. I made it. Link by link and yard by yard. Would you know the weight and length of your own chain, Scrooge? It was as heavy as this and as long as this seven Christmases ago. Tonight yours is a heavy chain indeed!

Scrooge How do you know that?

Jacob I have watched you, for my sins!

Scrooge Speak comfort to me, Jacob.

Jacob Comfort you may get but not from me. It is not permitted for me to tell you more than this. In life, my spirit never roamed beyond the narrow limits of our money-changing hole but now travel I must – an eternal journey.

Scrooge You mean you have journied in this way for seven years?

Jacob No rest. No peace. Endless sorrow.

Scrooge You travel fast?

Jacob On the wings of the wind but always bound within this chain.

Scrooge But you were always a good man of business, Jacob.

Jacob Business? Mankind was my business. The common good was my business.

There is a heavy rattle of the chain.

To think I walked through crowds of my fellow creatures with my eyes turned downwards. If but my eyes had been lead to see the misery around me, which it was within my power to remove. But, like yours Scrooge, these eyes saw nothing.

Scrooge Don't be too hard on me, Jacob.

Jacob I came here tonight to warn you that you have yet a chance of escaping my fate.

Scrooge   You were always a good friend to me, Jacob.
Thankee.

Jacob   You will be haunted by three Ghosts.

Scrooge   That is the hope you mentioned?

Jacob   Yes.

Scrooge   Then I would sooner not.

Jacob   Without these visits you cannot hope to be saved
from the path I tread. Expect the first tomorrow
night when the clock strikes twelve. Expect the
second on the next night at the same hour.

Scrooge   Couldn't I take them all together and have it over,
Jacob?

Jacob   The third on the next when the last stroke of
twelve has ceased to vibrate.

Scrooge   But I don't want to be visited!

Jacob   Ebenezer. Come to the window. See for a moment
with my eyes and tell me what you see, man.

*Scrooge is lead forward to the window and looks
out amazed. We hear wailing music up until the
departure of Jacob Marley.*

Scrooge   Jacob! Oh.

Jacob   What do you see?

Scrooge   The night is full of phantoms, chained as you are.
And him! In my life I knew him.

Jacob   Which?

Scrooge   And him too! There! The ghost all bound with
chains and safes and heavy bank books. We did
business together. And there! That poor wretch. Is
that his fate for ever, Jabob?

*Jacob Marley is starting to walk backwards away
from Scrooge. But Scrooge does not look around.*

Jacob   It is. His and mine. What do you see, Ebenezer?

He speaks as he is departing.

Scrooge   A woman, Jacob. A poor wretched woman with a child, huddled in a doorway, a ragged cape round her against the chilling snow. The ghost reaches out to help, to offer some assistance but he cannot. His chain holds him back. Is this how you have spent seven years, Jacob? Oh dreadful punishment. Jacob? Jacob?

There is silence. Jacob Marley has gone. Scrooge looks around him, looks around the room not trusting his senses now. Then he looks out of the window.

The woman and child still there but no ghost. Drat the cheese. It is humbug.

We hear a sudden rattling of chains, far off. Scrooge dives for the bed with a scream and climbs inside. He blows out the candle.

Scene Three

The scene starts with music as Scrooge snores. Then we hear the sound of far-off church bells. (The bells that precede the chimes of midnight.)

Then the chimes. Scrooge wakes and counts the chimes from beneath the bed clothes. Lights come up in the bedroom area. Scrooge is still with the blanket over his head.

Scrooge   Four. Five.

There is a pause.

Ten. Eleven. Twelve. Twelve?

He throws the blanket off.

Can't be. Past two when I went to bed. Clock must be wrong.

He checks the timepiece at his bedside.

Lord, clock's correct. Why, it isn't possible. Can I have slept through the whole day and far into another night? Or is it possible that something has happened to the sun and that it is twelve at noon?

He thinks for a moment.

Scrooge, don't be a damned fool.

Scrooge gets down from the bed and comes down to the window.

Not a sound. Pitch-black. Streets deserted. Oh God, I've lost a day. Expect the first tomorrow when the clock strikes twelve. Oh.

He runs back to the bed.

It's a bad dream. Perhaps it's a bad dream.

He pulls up the covers.

Expect the first . . . Well, there's no Spirits here. Proves it was the cheese. Keep away. I'm asleep.

We hear the sound of rushing wind and bells. Scrooge throws himself under the covers.

Ohhhh

Flashing lights and the Ghost of Christmas Past enters.

Are you the Spirit whose coming was foretold to me?

Christmas Past   I am.

Scrooge   Who and what are you?

Christmas Past   I am the Ghost of Christmas Past.

Scrooge   Long past?

Christmas Past   Your past.

Scrooge   You look, if I may say so, Spirit, somewhat worn.

Christmas Past   I am the ghost of your past Christmases, Scrooge! It is you that has made me thus!

Scrooge   I am sorry. What business brings you here, Spirit?

Christmas Past   Your welfare.

Scrooge   If you cared for my welfare, Spirit, you'd go and leave me to sleep.

Christmas Past   No. I seek your reclamation. Come! Rise!

Scrooge   Spirit, leave me be. The weather is hard and I have a cold. It'll be gone in a day or so. Return then good Spirit but, meanwhile, leave me to sleep.

Christmas Past   Come!

Christmas Past holds out her robe and Scrooge is compelled to take hold of it. They move forward.

Scrooge   No, Spirit! I cannot fly!

Christmas Past   Tonight, Scrooge, you will.

Music and lights as Christmas Past and Scrooge fly.

Scrooge   We fly! Spirit, how? Look, I'm a bird. What's happening to me? And see! The night is gone and there the winter sun. And . . . and . . . good heavens, Spirit, I know this place. My father sent me away to school here. God, how many years ago?

Music brings him down to earth. Christmas Past moves apart from Scrooge. They are on terra firma.

The road to school! And . . . the old stile still there. And the conker tree. The conkers we got from that tree. I had a one hundred and tenner from that very tree. How do I remember that? Oh, Spirit.

Christmas Past   Your lip is trembling, Scrooge, and is that a tear upon your cheek?

Scrooge   Certainly not. 'Tis my cold. I believe I mentioned I had a cold. Makes my eyes water. Lead on, Spirit!

Christmas Past   You remember the way?

Scrooge   Remember it? I could walk it blindfold.

Christmas Past   Strange that you have forgotten it for so many years.

Music and sound mix. Music suggests a Christmas meeting on horseback and carts meeting at a church.

From offstage.

Carollers   All poor men and humble,
All lone men who stumble,
Come haste ye nor feel ye afraid.

They continue humming over Scrooge's lines.

Scrooge   Spirit, look! The bridge by the school. Those boys on ponies. It's Jack. The small one. Jack what's his name? And the farmer's boy. What a catapult he had. When all the other school boys went home for the Christmas holidays, Spirit, and I could not, they asked me to play with them, the village boys. Oh and there the village dog. Wilhelmina, who had her puppies in the school one Christmas Eve. Wilhelmina! Here, girl! I stole milk for those puppies. Jack! Charlie! It's me. Ebenezer. Spirit, they do not answer. Wilhelmina!

Christmas Past   These are but the shadows of things that have been. They have no consciousness of us.

Scrooge   Oh, do but look at the Christmas Parade,. Every cart for miles used to meet at the empty school,

Spirit. There's Jenny and Albert. I sat with her on that cart one year. For just a moment. But still – a moment. And Albert, the fattest boy in the village. The human doughnut. And the twins!

Christmas Past   The school is not quite deserted.

Young Scrooge has entered with a picture book.

A solitary child abandoned by his father.

Scrooge is sobbing.

Scrooge   I know it.

Scrooge goes and takes the young boy by the shoulders.

Christmas Past   Your father never forgave you, Scrooge, for living while your mother died giving birth to you.

Scrooge   Poor boy.

Christmas Past   He cannot see or feel you, Scrooge. This abandoned boy is but a shadow as the others were.

Scrooge   Yes, but do not think this boy is quite alone, Spirit. Why look. There at the window. It's Ali Baba.

Young Scrooge looks up from his book.

He came on Christmas Eve, I assure you.

Young Scrooge waves his hand.

Ali Baba and what's his name, asleep at the gates of Damascus. Don't you see them? And the Sultan's groom turned upside down by the genie with the lamp. There he is standing on his head. Serve him right. What business has he, married to a princess?

There is a pause. Scrooge weeps.

Poor boy. Poor boy. I wish . . .

He dries his eyes.

. . . but it's too late now.

Christmas Past   What's the matter?

Scrooge   Nothing. Nothing. There were some carol singers at my door last night. I should have liked to have given them something, that's all.

Music starts.

Christmas Past   Let us see another Christmas. The boy still wanders the empty school every day of every holiday.

Young Scrooge gets up and walks around. Scrooge and Christmas Past go to one side.

From offstage.

May Scrooge   Ebenezer. Ebenezer.

Young Scrooge   May! May!

May, Young Scrooge's sister, enters.

May! May! You have come. How?

May Scrooge   I have come to bring you home, little brother.

Young Scrooge   Home?

May Scrooge   I have told father that if you are not allowed home at Christmas then I will not come either. Ebenezer, he's sent me to fetch you.

Young Scrooge   May!

May Scrooge   Ebenezer, we'll be together all Christmas long.

Young Scrooge   Home. Hurrah!

Scrooge   Oh May! May!

Christmas Past   Never a strong girl.

Scrooge   No.

Christmas Past   A delicate creature whom a breath might have withered. But she had a strong heart.

Scrooge   Oh she had. Oh she had.

Christmas Past   She died too in childbirth and had, I think, a child.

Scrooge   No more.

Christmas Past   Your nephew. Fred.

Scrooge   No more, Spirit. No more!

Christmas Past   Come another Christmas far from here. Take hold.

> *Music theme for the flying. Scrooge grasps the robe of Christmas Past.*

Scrooge   How many years do we travel, Spirit? And to where?

Christmas Past   Look down, Scrooge. Surely it is known to you?

Scrooge   Why, there's St Paul's and the whole City spread out beneath. Aghhhh.

> *With a sound change, they are falling. Scrooge falls to the ground. He gets up and brushes himself.*

Where are we?

Christmas Past   Here's a warehouse door.

Scrooge   There I am with – Oh.

> *Dick Wilkins and teenage Scrooge walk through with aprons on over their suits, carrying boxes marked 'Produce of India'. They hum 'God Rest Ye Merry Gentlemen' together happily. They exit as . . .*
>
> *Speaking from offstage.*

Mr Fezziwig   Music. We must have music. Where are those idle fiddlers?

Scrooge   Mr Fezziwig! Know it, Spirit? I was apprenticed here.

Mr Fezziwig enters with drinks. Mrs Fezziwig follows behind.

Mr Fezziwig   Come, Sirs.

He speaks to the musicians.

This will oil your fingers and your throats. My apprentices are dancers, I assure you.

Scrooge   Old Mr Fezziwig and Mrs F. Bless their hearts. There never was a better master or a better mistress. I'd punch any man on the nose who dared to say they were not!

Mrs Fezziwig   Dick! Ebenezer!

Mr Fezziwig and Mrs Fezziwig have a quick cuddle as we hear the sound of running feet. Teenage Scrooge and Dick Wilkins re-enter.

Scrooge   Dick Wilkins! Bless me. Dear Dick. A master at shove-ha'penny, Spirit. I never saw his like.

Mrs Fezziwig   Come lads. No more work tonight, eh Dad?

Mr Fezziwig   Indeed not. Christmas Eve, my dandies. Christmas Eve.

He gives them a hug.

All work . . .

Teenage Scrooge and Dick Wilkins   . . . and no play . . .

All and Scrooge   . . . makes Jack a dull boy!

They take off their aprons while speaking these lines.

Mr Fezziwig   And never a truer word spoken by the philosophers of Greece, of Rome, and of the Elephant and Castle. Come lads, let's have those shutters up before you can say Jack Robinson. The music is going to waste.

They tear off as the others come in and start dancing. Belle enters and stands apart. Elsie enters.

Scrooge Oh, wonderful. And she . . . there! The girl from the warehouse across the road. Skinflint never gave a Christmas party there. Mr Fezziwig insisted she come to us.

Teenage Scrooge comes back with Dick Wilkins. They are now in their suits. Dick Wilkins starts dancing with the newly arrived Elsie. Teenage Scrooge goes silently to ask Belle to dance. They dance. The Fezziwigs are dancing more robustly than anyone. Mr Fezziwig stops dancing.

Mr Fezziwig Don't stop your dancing but . . .

They do all stop.

Thank you. My friends, I have a speech to make.

Cheers.

Thank you. My speech is this. Merry Christmas.

Cheers.

Merry Christmas and my hearty thanks for all your work this year.

All More!

Mr Fezziwig I close my speech.

Applause. The applause dies away as Mr Fezziwig holds his hands up and shakes his head modestly. Scrooge goes on clapping after the others. The dance is taken up again. This time it is a formal set piece with six participants. At the end of it Dick Wilkins and Teenage Scrooge come together.

Teenage Scrooge Was there ever a dancer like our Master?

Dick Wilkins Never. Not even on the stage.

Teenage Scrooge And Mrs F?

Dick Wilkins   She is perfection.

Teenage Scrooge   I shall never leave here.

Dick Wilkins   Nor I.

> *The dance continues and ends with applause all round. All but Mr Fezziwig gather round the drinks table.*

Christmas Past   A small matter to make these silly folk so full of gratitude.

Scrooge   Small?

> *Stepping forward to toast.*

Teenage Scrooge   Mr Fezziwig!

All   Mr Fezziwig!

Christmas Past   Why? Is it not? He has spent but a few pounds of your mortal money. Three or four pounds perhaps. Is that so much that he deserves all this praise?

Scrooge   It isn't that, Spirit. He has the power to make us happy or unhappy. He chooses to make us happy and the happiness he gives is quite as great as if it cost a fortune.

> *Scrooge stops and looks at the Ghost of Christmas Past and at the beaming Mr Fezziwig.*

Christmas Past   What's the matter?

Scrooge   Nothing particular.

Christmas Past   Something, I think.

Scrooge   No. No. I should like to be able to say something to my clerk, Bob Cratchit, just now. That's all.

> *The music has finished.*

Mr Fezziwig   Come, the buffet is laid in the office. Eat your fill. For the Punch and Judy comes at seven.

Cheers are heard as the dancers leave, leaving Teenage Scrooge and Belle.

Christmas Past   You were happy here?

Scrooge   Oh yes.

Christmas Past   You loved her?

Teenage Scrooge places a ring on Belle's finger.

Scrooge   Oh, Spirit.

Christmas Past   Come then. We must see another Christmas. Later by two years.

Looking very agitated.

Scrooge   Two – no. Mercy, good Spirit!

Christmas Past   Your own London offices now, Scrooge. Your fiancée, this same lovely girl.

Scrooge   Spare me this. Spare me this!

Belle and Teenage Scrooge have moved apart.

Teenage Scrooge   Why do you say I have changed? I have not. At least I have not changed towards you.

Belle   Once you told me that Mr Fezziwig was the most kindly employer you ever wished to have and you would take him as your model in everything. Do your clerks look on you as you looked on him?

Teenage Scrooge   Fezziwig was a fool. A pleasant fool. But a fool nonetheless.

Scrooge   Some respect, Sir, if you please! Mr Fezziwig was twice the man you'll ever be.

Scrooge catches himself. He is shocked by his outburst.

Teenage Scrooge   I have not changed towards you, Belle. Why do you condemn a man merely because he wishes to make himself rich?

Belle Ebenezer, I have seen all your ideals fall away one by one.

Teenage Scrooge I have grown wiser – yes. But I am not changed towards you, am I? Am I?

Belle We were engaged when you were poor and content to be so. You were another man.

Teenage Scrooge I was a boy.

Belle With this ring you made me a promise. I release you from that promise.

Scrooge Nooooooooooo.

Teenage Scrooge Have I ever sought release?

Belle In words, no.

Teenage Scrooge In what then?

Belle In everything. Two years ago you asked a poor girl for her hand in marriage. Would you do so now? A poor girl? Poor family?

Teenage Scrooge You think not?

Belle How can I think that you would? You who now weigh everything in sovereigns and pence? And therefore I break our engagement.

Scrooge No. No. Spirit!

Belle I do it for the love of the man you once were.

Scrooge You damn puppy! She's leaving you, man! She was the only one you ever loved! Blast you! Turn your face! Look at what you lose, man! Look! Spirit!

Belle May you be happy with the life you have chosen.

As Belle goes.

Scrooge Go after her, you young fool, why don't you?

He weeps.

Why don't you?

As Teenage Scrooge goes.

Spirit, show me no more. Why do you delight to torture me?

Christmas Past One shadow more.

Scrooge No more!

Christmas Past Many years have passed. This same girl, now long and happily married, the girl you had so quickly forgotten, still had a kind thought for you.

Belle enters on Christmas Eve.

Scrooge I do not wish to see it. No more!

Belle's husband, Charlie, enters in a Father Christmas suit. He has a small child asleep in his arms. Belle laughs.

Belle Charlie! What are you doing up with little Charlie? It's past midnight.

Charlie Shh. I couldn't help it, Mum. I was putting the stockings at the foot of the bed. This one ups, still asleep, and grabs the beard, if you please.

Belle Ah.

Charlie Strong glue, you know. Wouldn't give way. I cried out. He woke up. Straight way asked why Father Christmas had taken so long to get from the North Pole to Hackney Wick? Most indignant that I hadn't arrived before he fell asleep.

Belle But what did you say?

Charlie Told little Charlie that the Christmas Elves in Greenland had given me some very slow reindeer this year.

Belle Merry Christmas, Charlie.

She embraces him.

Charlie Merry Christmas, Belle.

Scrooge   Spirit, take me away, I beg you.

Charlie   Belle, I saw an old friend of yours this afternoon.

Belle   Who?

Charlie   Mr Scrooge. I passed his office window. His partner Marley lies upon the point of death, I hear, and there Scrooge sat alone. Quite alone in the world I believe.

Belle   Poor man.

Charlie embraces Belle and they slowly exit.

Scrooge   Spirit, remove me from this place.

Christmas Past   I told you these were the shadows of the things that have been. That they are what they are, do not blame me.

Scrooge   Remove me. I cannot bear it.

Music begins. Scrooge breaks down.

I cannot bear it.

Christmas Past moves away as the music rises. Scrooge is not looking at her.

Haunt me no longer!

Christmas Past disappears. The music becomes less loud and there is silence at last. Scrooge looks around and finds himself in his own room. He finds his way wearily to his bed.

Haunt me no longer. Let me sleep, I beg you.

Scrooge drags himself into bed and pulls up the covers. Scrooge sleeps.

Scene Four

Music starts and is then mixed with the sound of bells. There is a pause and then silence.

*Then the sound of the bell starting to strike twelve.
Scrooge starts to wake. He listens.*

Scrooge Twelve o'clock on the second night, that's what
Jacob said. Alright, come on, whoever you are. I'm
ready for you. You won't take me by surprise this
time.

*Silence. Scrooge gets out of the bed and looks
around. He looks under the bed. There is nothing
there.*

There. Not coming.

A chord of music. All the lights go out briefly.

Aghh. Mercy! Mercy!

*The lights come up. Dazzling lights on the ghost of
Christmas Present. Scrooge covers his eyes.*

Christmas Present   Ebenezer Scrooge. I am the ghost of
Christmas Present. Look upon me.

Scrooge Spirit, leave me be, I beg you. I cannot endure
such another night as your fellow Spirit offered
me. The past is past. I cannot change it. And I
cannot change. Mercy, Spirit, leave me to sleep.

*The distant sound of carols is heard. It continues
through the scene at low level.*

Carollers Here we come, we come.
A Happy New Year, we come, we come.

Christmas Present   Ah. There is a sound after my own heart.
Do you hear it, Scrooge?

Scrooge I hear it, Spirit, but have forgotten the words.

Carollers Bring us out a table and spread it with a cloth,
Bring us out some mouldy cheese,
And some of your Christmas loaf.
Lalala.

They continue humming.

Christmas Present   Scrooge, is this how you treat your Christmas guests? Come, man, have you no festive fare to offer?

Scrooge   I regret I have not, Spirit. I do not make merry at Christmas.

Christmas Present   What? No flask about you. No mince pies? No Christmas cake? Wine?

Scrooge shakes his head.

Scrooge   I regret not, Spirit.

Christmas Present   Scrooge! Scrooge! We have a long day before us. We must see all that this great day offers. Every sight. But we cannot begin it without something to fortify us. Come, man, you will join me in making merry!

Scrooge   But I do not know how, Spirit!

Starting to exit in the direction of the bar.

Christmas Present   Then I will teach you, man! Come! I smell mince pies in that direction.

Scrooge   Spirit!

Christmas Present exits followed by Scrooge. The carolling group have come on stage.

Narrator   My young friends, we are going to follow the good ghost's festive example and refresh ourselves. Perhaps you would care to do the same. The sweet meats await.

Carollers   Bring us out a table,
And spread it with a cloth.
Bring us out some mouldy cheese,
And some of your Christmas loaf,
Love and joy come to you,
And to our wassail too.

And God bless you and send you,
A Happy New Year.

They begin to exit the stage area still singing.

Call up the butler of this house,
Put on his golden ring.
Let him bring us a glass of beer,
And better we shall sing.
Love and joy come to you,
And to our wassail too.
And God bless you and send you,
A Happy New Year.

The carol fades on their exit. The house lights go up.
Interval.

ACT TWO

Scene One

The Carollers enter playing a round of handbells.

Scrooge Down there, Spirit. The parade of carollers. Is this Christmas morning?

Christmas Present It is.

Carollers God rest you merry gentlemen,
Let nothing you dismay.
For Jesus Christ our saviour,
Was born on Christmas Day,
To save us all from Satan's power,
When we have gone astray.
Oh tidings of comfort and joy, comfort and joy,
Oh tidings of comfort and joy.

They end with a cheer.

Merry Christmas.

The carollers exit. Three break off to take on the parts of Mrs Cratchit, Martha Cratchit and Belinda Cratchit. The Cratchit house scene is already set.

Christmas Present Before you is the poor house of one Bob Cratchit. Poor but very rich.

Mrs Cratchit What is keeping your poor father? And your brother, Tiny Tim? And Martha wasn't as late last Christmas by half an hour.

Entering.

Martha Here's Martha, Mother!

Belinda Martha! Martha! Hurrah! Martha, Mother has bought a goose.

She whispers to Martha.

Remark how big it is when you are shown it. And the pudding too.

Mrs Cratchit   Why bless your heart alive, my dear. How late you are!

They kiss and hug each other.

Taking off shawl.

Martha   There was a deal of work to finish up at the factory last night, Ma, and we had to clear up this morning.

Mrs Cratchit   Making you clear up on Christmas morning? I've never heard of such a thing. Even . . . Well, never mind him! Never mind anything as long as you've come. Sit down before the fire, my dear, and have a warm.

Bob Cratchit can be heard singing. He is approaching the house.

Belinda   No. No. Here's Father coming. Hide, Martha.

Martha hides.

Singing from offstage.

Cratchit   There was a pig went out to dig,
Christmas Day, Christmas Day.
There was a pig went out to dig,
On Christmas Day in the morning.

Entering.

There was a cow went out to plough,
Christmas Day, Christmas Day.
There was a cow went out to plough
Christmas Day in the morning.

Bob Cratchit enters with Tiny Tim on his shoulder. Tiny Tim carries a crutch. Tim is put down.

Why, where's our Martha?

Mrs Cratchit   Not coming.

Cratchit   Not coming. Not coming on Christmas Day?

Bob Cratchit's face drops. So does Tiny Tim's.
Martha Cratchit reacts quickly and shows herself.
There is great relief. They hug each other.

Martha   Tim, will you show me the goose?

Tiny Tim   I will. I will.

Tiny Tim puts his arms up to be lifted by Martha
Cratchit.

Martha and Belinda take one arm each and swing
him gently off.

Mrs Cratchit   Martha not here on Christmas Day? Get on with
you, Bob Cratchit. She wouldn't miss this day for
all the world.

Cratchit   I know it. I know it.

Mrs Cratchit   And how did little Tim behave in church?

Cratchit   As good as gold and better. Oh, but Mother, he
says the strangest things.

Mrs Cratchit   What was it today, Bob?

Cratchit   Well, my dear. In church, Tim's crutch was leaning
against a pew. Then, by accident, a lady knocked it
to the floor. She picked it up and then, well . . . she
just looked at it a long while.

Mrs Cratchit   Why, Bob?

Cratchit   That's what I asked Tim. He thought for a moment
and then he said, perhaps the lady was thinking,
seeing the crutch, of the man whose birthday it is
today who made lame children walk.

Mrs Cratchit reacts. She knows there will be no
such miracle. And worse.

Scrooge   Oh, Spirit, I did not know.

Christmas Present   Did you ever seek to know?

Cratchit   But he mends, my dear. He mends. He grows stronger by the day. And such a weight.

Scrooge   Is this true, Spirit?

Bob Cratchit's statement is not convincing and we should see that Mrs Cratchit is not convinced. She attempts not to show this to her husband. Mrs Cratchit is suddenly very low. There is a pause. Tiny Tim enters with Martha behind. Martha Cratchit has a small tray with a set of cups and a bowl.

Is it true, Spirit?

No response.

Tiny Tim   My lords, ladies and gentlemen, the punch!

Martha holds up the punch.

Attempting to lift Mrs Cratchit's spirits.

Cratchit   The punch?

She nods and gets up.

All   The punch.

Cratchit   Looks fit for the Lord Mayor himself.

Mrs Cratchit   The Lord Mayor can buy his own. How looks the goose, Tim?

Tiny Tim   It looks as big as me.

Mrs Cratchit   Go on with you. You don't think it's too small for all of us? It's more stuffing than goose.

Cratchit   The goose? Huge, Tim?

Tiny Tim   Huge, Father.

Cratchit   Feed a regiment, Tim?

Tiny Tim   Two regiments, Father, and the Navy too.

Cratchit (to Mrs Cratchit)   There.

To Tiny Tim.

And the pudding, Sir? Will it go round?

Tiny Tim And around and around till we burst.

Mrs Cratchit It's a very small pudding.

Cratchit Tim?

Bob Cratchit holds his hands out to indicate a small pudding. Tiny Tim hobbles over and slowly, one hand at a time, pushes both of Bob's hands to their farthest extent. Everyone is laughing at 'the huge pudding'.

My dears, a toast.

He picks up Tim.

Come, my young shaver.

He brings him to the head of the table.

A merry Christmas to us all, my dears. God bless us.

All A merry Christmas.

Tiny Tim God bless us, every one.

All take a drink.

Scrooge Spirit, tell me if Tiny Tim will live.

Christmas Present I see a vacant seat in the chimney corner and a crutch without an owner, carefully preserved in memory. If these shadows remain unaltered by the future the child will die.

Scrooge Oh no. No, kind Spirit. Say he will be spared.

Christmas Present If these shadows remain unaltered by the future, none of my kind will find him here.

Scrooge No. No!

Christmas Present What then? If he be like to die, he had better do it and decrease the surplus population.

Scrooge   Noooooooooo.

Christmas Present   Man, if man you be in heart, do you know
what the surplus is and where it is? Will you
decide what men shall live and what men shall
die? It may that in the sight of heaven, you are
worth less, and less fit to live than millions like this
poor man's child.

Scrooge is totally cast down.

Cratchit   Mr Scrooge. I give you Mr Scrooge, the founder of
the feast.

*Everyone reacts in their own way to the offer of the
toast. Cups which are almost at the lips are put
down, etc.*

Mrs Cratchit   Founder of the feast indeed! I wish I had him
here. I'd give him a piece of my mind to feast upon
and I hope he'd have a good appetite for it.

Cratchit   My dear. The children! Christmas Day.

Mrs Cratchit   It should be Christmas Day, I'm sure, on which
one drinks the health of such an odious, stingy,
hard, unfeeling man as Mr Scrooge. You know he
is, Bob. Nobody knows it better than you, poor
fellow.

Cratchit   My dear, Christmas Day.

Mrs Cratchit   I'll drink his health for your sake and the day's.
Not for his. Long life to him. A merry Christmas
and a happy New Year. He'll be very merry and
very happy I have no doubt.

*At last they raise their cups unwillingly. They stop
and Bob wordlessly begs them to complete the
toast. They drink.*

Cratchit   Come, Tim, my young sportsman, I noticed some
shavers have made a handsome slide down at the

corner. Let's go and have a quick shoot down it before dinner. What do you say?

Tiny Tim   Yes, Father!

Tiny Tim shoots his arms up to be taken.

As the room is cleared.

All   There was a pig went out to dig
Christmas Day, Christmas Day.
There was a pig went out to dig,
Christmas Day in the morning.

Bob takes Tim and exits. He is followed by the girls, waving.

There was a sparrow went out to harrow,
Christmas Day, Christmas Day.
There was a sparrow went out to harrow,
Christmas Day in the morning.

Fade the carol as required by their exit.

Scene Two

Scrooge and Christmas Present are left alone.

Christmas Present   Come, take my robe. You still have much to see and little time.

Scrooge   Spirit, I am ready.

Music. Scrooge closes his eyes. Music mixes into the sound of the cold winter wind. Mix in the sound of the Christmas song with wind, sung by rough voices.

Carollers   'Twas Christmas Eve and down the pit,
The miners' lamps were all still lit.
When a voice rang out through the dirt and grit,
Noel to miners everywhere.

They continue humming.

Scrooge   What place is this, Spirit?

Christmas Present   This is a place where coal miners live. Behold them, Scrooge. Though they have spent all year below ground, men, women and children, all bent double with their cruel labour, though they have little to rejoice in, see, hear them now at Christmas. In every heart a kindly thought.

Scrooge   I see them, Spirit.

Christmas Present   See them then and learn. Come! Away!

Music plays again. Eerie sounds as Scrooge grabs the cloak of Christmas Present. Sound of waves breaking on rocks. High winds.

Scrooge   No. No, good Spirit. Do not take me over the sea! I cannot swim.

Christmas Present   You are safe, Scrooge. See in yon lighthouse, the men who guard the light to keep all seamen safe. Though their lonely work strips them from family, friends and children, see.

Scrooge   I hear them, Spirit.

Christmas Present   Look into their hearts and see Christmas there, and then, Scrooge, look into your own.

Scrooge   Spirit, I do.

Christmas Present   Come, further out to sea.

Scrooge   No, Spirit! No!

Carollers   I saw three ships come sailing by,
On Christmas Day, Christmas Day,
I saw three ships come sailing by,
On Christmas Day in the morning.

Scrooge has grabbed hold of the robe again. We hear the sound of sea gales. Creaking ship's timbers.

Speaking over carol.

Christmas Present   See below, Scrooge. See yon mariners as their ship challenges the mighty ocean. There, the helmsman at the wheel, the officer who has the watch. And every man on board has a kinder word on this day than any other day of the year.

Scrooge nods.

Scene Three

We hear the sound of Fred Scrooge's laugh offstage.

Christmas Present   Come. We have one last place to visit. A place where you are thought of, Scrooge.

Music continues through this as Fred Scrooge, Mrs Fred Scrooge, Tupper, Florence and others enter.

Fred   Ha ha ha. He said that Christmas was a humbug. As I live, he believed it too!

Mrs Fred   More shame for him, Fred.

All   Shame!

Fred   No, he's a comical old fellow. I couldn't be angry with him if I tried. Who suffers by his whims? Him always. He takes it into his head to dislike us and he won't come and dine with us. What's the consequence? He don't lose much of a dinner.

Fred Scrooge ducks as Mrs Fred Scrooge takes a swipe at him.

Catching him.

Mrs Fred   What sort of a dinner does he lose?

Fred   A good one, my dear.

She twists his ear.

Not good. Excellent.

Another twist.

Not excellent. Superb.

Releasing him with a flourish.

Mrs Fred   Thank you.

General laughter.

Fred   In any event, I mean to give him the same chance every year to come to dinner here, whether he likes it or not.

Tupper   Fred, if your uncle were to come here today upon your invitation, I would put a tenner in his skinflint claw. I would.

Fred   Oh, you're too hard. No, I will try again next year.

Scrooge   Thank you, Fred. Thank you kindly.

Fred   And now, my friend Tupper has requested a game of blind man's buff!

Party guest   Yes, and we know why.

Tupper, through this scene, has been making ill-disguised glances at a certain blushing girl, Florence. She will shortly become the sole object of his blindfold chase. This is of no surprise to the guests. Fred has taken out his own kerchief. He binds Tupper's eyes with it.

Fred   Yes, Tupper has very kindly volunteered himself to be the first blind man.

Mrs Fred   Tie him up tight, Fred!

Scrooge   Give him a good spin, Fred!

Fred   Are you blind, Tupper? Tell me as gentleman.

Tupper   Can't see a thing, Fred.

Cries of disbelief from the company.

Party guest Pull the other one, Tupper.

Scrooge Don't believe him, Spirit.

Fred Scrooge spins Tupper round to the cheers of the others. Then Tupper is let loose. A pause and then he immediately heads for the chosen girl, Florence.

He can see! The young jackanapes.

Party guest Disgraceful!

Party guests are getting in Tupper's way.

Scrooge Oh, I remember something similar. Dick Wilkins was just such a wag.

Mrs Fred Fred, he can see!

One of the party goes and put themselves in the way of Tupper's advance on Florence. Tupper avoids this obstacle and continues to chase Florence. Further cries.

Scrooge He surpasses Dick Wilkins, this fellow. The young pup. Is he not a pup, Spirit?

Party guest Tupper, those hands, Sir, if you please!

Scrooge To think if I had taken Fred's invitation, Spirit, all these years they would perhaps have allowed me to chase the girls.

Tupper catches Florence. There is a hush over the room.

Tupper Now let me guess who this is.

Party guest Guess? You know who it is very well, you dog!

Tupper This could take a little while.

He starts to feel at the girl's waist. She blushes. Fred Scrooge steps in and removes Tupper's blindfold.

Fred	See who you have caught, Tupper.
Tupper	Well I never did!
Party guest	Oh really?
Fred	Never?
	As all laugh.
Scrooge	I haven't enjoyed myself so much in years. Let's have another game.
Fred	Let's have another game.
All and Scrooge	Yes. Yes.
Fred	What will it be?
Christmas Present	Scrooge!
Scrooge	A few more moments, Spirit.
Mrs Fred	'Yes and No'.
All	Agreed!
Fred	Very well. 'Yes and No' it is. Now I am thinking of something. You may question me but I may only answer yes or no.
Scrooge	A pancake? St Paul's Cathedral. A Christmas pudding?
	There is a pause. He announces with certainty.
	An African giraffe.
Mrs Fred	Is it in this room?
Fred	No.
Party guest	Is it in London?
Fred	Yes.
All	Hurrah.
Scrooge	Still could be the giraffe. The one at the zoo.
Party guest	Is it a building?
Fred	No.

Tupper	Is it a street? Is it this street?
Fred	No and no.
Tupper	A district?
Fred	No.
Scrooge	No. No. No. You're on the wrong track, nitwits!
Mrs Fred	Is it alive?
Fred	Yes.
All	Hurrah.
Scrooge	The giraffe. I knew it. He always loved giraffes.
Party guest	Is it an animal?
Fred	Yes.
Party guest	A wild animal?
Fred	Yes.
Scrooge	Come on, you dozies, it's the giraffe. Why don't you listen?
Mrs Fred	A tiger?
Fred	No.
Party guest	A leopard?
Fred	No.
Tupper	A duck-billed platypus?
Party guest	A what?
Fred	No.
Mrs Fred	A snake? An alligator? Shark? Tupper's dog, Billy?
Fred	No, no, no and no.
Party guest	A bear?
	Fred Scrooge shakes his head.
	A bull? Ape? Boar?
Fred	No.

Mrs Fred	This is not a friendly animal?
Fred	No. Pleasant? No.
Tupper	A wombat?
Party guest	Pardon?
Fred	No.
Party guest	Is it led on a chain?
Fred	No.
Scrooge	It's a giraffe. An African giraffe! How many more times?
Tupper	I know!

There is a pause.

I have it, Fred. Your favourite. I have it. An African giraffe.

Scrooge	At last.

He slaps Tupper on the back.

Has brains this Tupper. My turn.

Fred	No.

Scrooge is dumbfounded.

Mrs Fred	A wild animal, an unpleasant animal, lives in London, is not led around on a chain. A human animal?
Fred	Yes.
Mrs Fred	A human animal that talks?
Fred	Occasionally. Yes, I should say.
Mrs Fred	Roams around London uncaged?
Fred	Yes.
Mrs Fred	I have it, Fred.
Fred	Then what is it?

Mrs Fred It's your Uncle Scrooge. Correct?

Fred It is. I confess it.

General applause.

Tupper Then, Fred, I must protest.

Scrooge Thank you, Tupper.

Fred On what score, Tupper?

Tupper On two scores, Frederick. Your answer to 'Is it a bear?' was 'No'. Your answer to 'Is it a boar?' was 'No'. Well, I call that stretching the truth.

They laugh as music begins. Scrooge is very disappointed at the outcome of the game.

Fred Well, boar or not, he has given us plenty of merriment, I'm sure, so let's go in and drink his health and then we dance. We'll wish a Merry Christmas to the old man whereever he is. He wouldn't take it from me but he'll take it from all of us nonetheless.

Exiting.

All To Uncle Scrooge!

Pause. Ebenezer Scrooge starts to grunt and snort.

Scrooge A bear? Ha ha. A boar? Ha ha.

Scene Four

Scrooge looks around and sees Christmas Present. She indicates to him that it is long past the time to depart.

Christmas Present Come, there is still much to see.

Scrooge nods. A Narrator enters. (In the following carols, heavy type denotes that the carol is sung loud at these points.)

Narrator

Scrooge and his Spirit were again on their travels. Much they saw and many homes they visited. The Spirit stood beside sickbeds and they were cheerful, on foreign lands and they were close to home, by struggling men and they were patient and still in hope, by poverty and it was rich.

In poor-house, hospital, and prison, wherever the hand of man had not barred the door to Christmas, there they were and Scrooge learned its meaning.

Overlap carols.

It was a long night if it was only a night, but Scrooge had his doubts about this because they travelled through all twelve days of Christmas leaving at last a children's twelfth Night party. Scrooge saw that time for the Spirit's departure had come. Scrooge was troubled.

Carollers

Dans cette étable
Que Jésus est charmant
Qu'il est aimable
Dans cet abaissement!
**Que d'attraits à la fois
Tous les palais des rois**
N'ont rien de comparable
(*Starts to fade.*)
Aux charmes que je vois
Dans cette étable.

Carollers

**Veinticinco de Diciembre
Fum, fum, fum
Nacido ha por nuestro amor**
El niño dios.
El niño dios (*Start to fade.*)
Hoy de la Virgen Maria
En esta noche tan fría
Fum, fum, fum.

Carollers

Stille Nacht, heilige Nacht
Alles schläft, einsam wacht
Nur das traute,
Hochheilige Paar,
Holder Knabe im
Lockigem Haar
Schlaf' in himmlischer Ruh'
Schlaf' in himmlischer Ruh'.

Scrooge Are Spirits' lives so short?

Christmas Present My life upon this globe is very brief. It ends tonight.

Scrooge Tonight?

Christmas Present Tonight at midnight.

Scrooge Spirit, forgive me if I am not justified in what I ask, but in our travels I have begun to see beneath your robe something which horrifies me. Forgive me, but two children, a girl and a boy, clinging to you. Wretched, disfigured, hideous children. Spirit, are the little ones yours?

Christmas Present   They are man's but they cling to me. The boy is Ignorance and the girl is Need.

The children come from the robe and move towards Scrooge.

Scrooge   No, Spirit, do not show me!

Christmas Present   Never again turn your back on their existence, Scrooge. Not on the boy, Ignorance, nor on this girl, Need.

Scrooge   Spirit, will no one help you in your good work? Will no one take them in?

A beat sounds.

Christmas Present   Are there no prisons?

The first chime of midnight sounds.

Are there no workhouses?

The second chime sounds and then on to twelve as Christmas Present departs with the children.

Scene Five

Scrooge is utterly cast down. Church bells become distorted and a slight mist begins to rise. Chilling music as a hooded robed figure starts slowly to enter. It should have a blind man's mask hooding its eyes. If we see anything it is only the mouth. From the robe a thin finger beckons.

Scrooge   I am in the presence of Christmas yet to come?

There is a pause but no reply.

You are about to show me shadows of future happenings?

Another pause. No answer.

Is that so, Spirit? Ghost of the Future, I fear you more than any spectre I have seen. But as I hope to live a better man, I am prepared to bear your company. But you will not speak to me? Show me the future then. The night is waning fast and it is precious time to me, I know.

A gesture from the Spirit. We begin to hear distant voices from the Stock Exchange. Two Stockbrokers appear with stock papers held high.

First Stockbroker   Midland and Scottish Railways. Sovereign a share. Buy. Buy.

Second Stockbroker   Empire Goldfields. Five shillings and sixpence. Sell. Sell.

Scrooge   Are we in the City, Spirit? The Stock Exchange? I only half recognise it. It is in some way strange to me. If this were the Exchange, I would be standing over there but I am not.

First Stockbroker   I don't know much about it. I only know he's . . .

Second Stockbroker   When?

First Stockbroker   Last night.

Second Stockbroker   What was the matter with him? I thought he'd last for . . .

Another stockbroker enters.

First Stockbroker   God knows.

The first two stockbrokers look at the third.

Third Stockbroker   How are you?

First Stockbroker   How are you?

Second Stockbroker   Old Scratch has . . .

Third Stockbroker   So I'm told.

First Stockbroker   Snuff?

Third Stockbroker   Thank you.

Second Stockbroker   What has he done with his . . .?

First Stockbroker   I haven't heard. He hasn't left me anything, that's all I know.

Third Stockbroker   Are you going to the . . .?

First Stockbroker   No. Too miserable. Don't like those affairs. Unless, of course, there's a free lunch provided.

Second Stockbroker   Free lunch? Old Scratch? Quite out of character.

Third Stockbroker   Then there'll be no one there. That I do know.

They laugh, hand each other share papers and begin to exit.

Third Stockbroker   Kimberley Diamonds. Eleven and six. Buy. Buy.

Second Stockbroker   Consolidated Copper. At six shillings. Sell. Sell.

First Stockbroker   Midland and Scottish Railways. At a sovereign. Buy.

They have exited.

Scrooge   Spirit, of whom were they speaking? I have had to do with each of them through business. Is it Jacob Marley they speak of, Spirit? Answer me!

A gesture from the Spirit. Music and sounds of a busy street: dogs barking, babies crying.

Spirit, where am I now? I do not know this part of the city. It is foul, Spirit. Take me away, I beg you.

A woman, Mrs Delaney, enters with a cart full of rags. She has a bundle over her shoulder.

Mrs Delaney   Rag-a-bone! Rag-a-bone!

Mrs Maggs enters with a bundle of rags chasing after.

Mrs Maggs   Mrs Delaney, wait on. I've got some merchandise if you're buying and it ain't no rags neither.

Mrs Delaney   Where does it come from?

Mrs Maggs   What does it matter where it comes from?

Mrs Delaney   I'll put it another way for you, dear. Where did you purloin it and whom did you purloin it off?

Mrs Maggs   What odds, eh? I'll tell you this. The bloke who owned it won't miss it.

Mrs Delaney   He won't?

Mrs Maggs   He's past missing anything. Get me?

Mrs Delaney   Here, this from that old man you clean for once a month?

Mrs Maggs   There. See me point? Anyone who's too mean to have his apartments cleaned more'an once a month don't deserve better. You agree?

Mrs Delaney   What you got?

Mrs Maggs starts to fish out the clothing and bedding. Mrs Delaney inspects it.

Mrs Maggs   If he's had a been any sort of a man he's had a had someone by his bedside when the grim reaper come for him. My point. He didn't have a friend in the world as far as I know.

She points to the clothing.

What do you think? Blankets still got some wear in 'em. The sheets are a bit – but they'll wash up with plenty of bleach. Now the bed curtains are good. The rings alone are worth five bob, I know.

Mrs Delaney   Mrs Maggs, you didn't?

Mrs Maggs   What?

Mrs Delaney   Didn't take these bed curtains down with the dead body still lying there, did you?

Mrs Maggs   Well, he hadn't been fetched.

Mrs Delaney   And himself lying in these sheets?

Mrs Maggs   Yes.

Mrs Delaney   Blimey, you've got some face.

Mrs Maggs   Look at this nightshirt. Now the rest of it, I agree. But that's a best nightshirt.

There is a pause.

They's had have wasted that, if it hadn't been for me.

Mrs Delaney   How do you mean?

Mrs Maggs   Some fool putting it on him to be buried in. Well, I had that off him. None of that.

Mrs Delaney   Mrs Maggs, I'll say this for you. You've got some face. Well, you'll have to come to the shop for a price on this collection. I need a second opinion.

They start to exit.

Here, he didn't die of no disease, did he?

Mrs Maggs   Not him! No self-respecting disease would have gone near him. No, he just outlived his welcome. Good riddance. The old miser.

They both exit.

Departing.

Mrs Delaney   Rag-a-bone! Rag-a-bone!

Scrooge   Spirit, I see. The case of this unhappy man might have been my own. My life tends that way now.

Sombre music plays and two pallbearers enter. They open up a grave on the stage (or bring in a coffin).

Merciful heaven!

One of the pallbearers offers the other a smoke. The Spirit points at the figure in the grave and implies that Scrooge must look into the grave. Scrooge draws back.

Spirit, let me go. This graveyard is a fearful place and I have learnt its lesson. Trust me.

Again the Spirit indicates for Scrooge to look at the grave.

I understand you and would do if I could but I have not the power, Spirit! Spirit, is there any tenderness connected with this man's death – ?

A gesture from the Spirit. Music plays as Mrs Cratchit and Martha enter. Some way behind them is Bob Cratchit.

Martha   Father walks a little slower than he used.

There is a pause. She looks round.

I have known him walk with – I have known him walk with Tiny Tim upon his shoulder very fast indeed.

Bob catches up with them. He carries flowers.

Mrs Cratchit   Bob, don't be grieved.

Bob kneels. They do so as well.

Cratchit   And he took a child and set him in the midst of them.

They make a silent prayer. As they do so, Fred Scrooge enters with a wreath. He stands by the grave. This startles Ebenezer Scrooge. The Cratchits notice him.

I met Mr Fred at the cemetery gates, my dear, and seeing that I looked just a little down, you know, he – I told him of our loss. 'I am heartily sorry for it, Mr Cratchit. If I can be of service to you in any way,' he said, giving me his card, 'pray come and see me.' It really seemed as if he had known Tim and felt with us.

Mrs Cratchit   I am sure he is a good soul.

Cratchit   And because he is, my dear, I will join him in his duty. Wait for me at the gate, my dears, will you?

They nod and exit. Bob joins Fred at the grave.

As the Spirit points to the grave

Scrooge   I fear I need not ask who is that man to be buried here, but before I draw nearer to that corpse – Spirit, are these the shadows of things that will be or are they the shadows of things that may be only?

The Spirit still points to the grave. Fred has placed his wreath upon the corpse. There is an inscription on the wreath. Scrooge approaches the wreath, then he reads.

In memoriam. Ebenezer Scrooge. I am the man here!

Funeral music plays and the coffin is removed by the pall bearers as Scrooge sinks to his knees. Fred and Bob exit.

No, Spirit. Oh no, Spirit. Hear me. I am not the man I was. I will not be the man I would have been without you and your fellow Spirits. Marley promised me a hope, but you appear to offer none. Spirit, why show me this if I am beyond all hope? Spirit, show me I may have hope.

The Spirit who has been unmovable, now seems to shake. He has been affected by Scrooge's words.

Good Spirit, I see you pity me! Promise me I may yet change these shadows by an altered life.

The Spirit trembles more.

I will honour Christmas in my heart and try to keep it all the year. I will live in the past, present and future. The Spirits of all three will live in me. I will not shut out the lessons you have taught me. Spirit, tell me I may live in hope.

The Spirit, unseen by Scrooge, has disappeared. Scrooge follows on his knees, desperate.

No!

By this time Scrooge has reached the bedroom area. The music dies away leaving him quietly sobbing.

Tell me I may live in hope! Tell me I may live in hope.

There is silence.

Scene Six

Carollers   God bless ye merry gentlemen.
Let nothing you dismay.

He has listened to the line of the carol. He sees that he is in his bedroom.

Scrooge   I'm alive! Oh Spirit, Spirit! I do live in hope. I will live in the past, present and future. Oh Jacob Marley, heaven and the Christmas Spirits be praised for this. I say it on my knees. The bed still here. The blankets. She didn't steal them. They are here. I am here. The shadows of things that would

have been can be dispelled. They will be. I know
they will. Hmmm. I don't know what to do. I'm as
light as a feather.

This as the Carollers enter looking at Scrooge.

Carollers   God rest ye merry gentlemen,
Let nothing you dismay,
For Jesus Christ our saviour,
Was born on Christmas Day.
To save us all from Satan's power,
When we had gone astray.
Oh tidings of comfort and joy, comfort and joy,
Oh tidings of comfort and joy.

Scrooge is dressing himself in his day clothes.

Scrooge   I am as merry as a schoolboy.

Scrooge continues dressing.

Carollers   God bless the ruler of this house,
And send him long to reign,
And many a merry Christmas,
May live to see again.
Among your friends and kindred,
That live both far and near,
And go send you a Happy New Year,
Send you a Happy New Year.

To the departing Carollers.

Scrooge   Merry Christmas. A Merry Christmas to everyone.
And a Happy New Year to all the world.

Scrooge looks around his room.

There's the door by which the Ghost of Jacob
Marley entered. There's the window where I saw
the poor wandering Spirits. I don't know what day
of the month it is. I don't know how long I've been
among the Spirits. Days at least. Perhaps weeks. I
don't know anything. Never mind. I don't care. I'd
rather be a baby.

Merry peals of bells sound and Scrooge goes to the window.

What a beautiful day. Sun. Oh golden sun. And snow!

A youngster enters front stage.

You, Sir. Young man. Young shaver in the street! What day is it?

Boy Eh?

Scrooge What day is it, my fine fellow?

Boy Today? Why Christmas Day.

Scrooge It's Christmas Day. I haven't missed it. The Spirits have done it all in one night. They can do anything they like. Of course they can. Of course they can. Hello, my fine fellow.

Boy Hello.

Scrooge Do you know the poulterers in the next street?

Boy I should hope I do.

Scrooge An intelligent boy. A remarkable boy. Do you know whether they've sold the prize turkey that was hanging up there – not the little prize turkey – the big one.

Boy What? The one as big as me?

Scrooge What a delightful boy. It's a pleasure to talk to him. Yes, my buck.

Boy It's hanging there now.

Scrooge Is it? Then go and buy it.

Boy Nutty.

Scrooge Go and inform the poulterer that I will purchase it. Stand by it till I come. I'll give you instructions where to take it. You'll take a cab of course and there'll be five shillings for yourself. Now what do you say? Will you run this errand, my fine herbert?

Boy   Run it? Five shillings? You watch me!

And the Boy runs off, whooping.

Scrooge   I'll send it to Bob Cratchit. He shan't know who sent it. It's twice the size of Tiny Tim.

He takes out the invitation from Fred, which is crumpled. He straightens it carefully.

I will –

He looks at his clothes.

But not in this. I'm off to the tailor. Yes, I am.

He starts to move but sees the approach of the two philanthropists.

Stop. Stop. I beg you, ladies. Please.

They stop and turn.

Ladies, I trust you gathered a great deal of money for the poor last night. A Merry Christmas, ladies.

First Philanthropist   Mr Scrooge?

Second Philanthropist   Mr Scrooge?

Scrooge   Yes, that is my name and I fear it may not be pleasant to you. Allow me to ask your pardon but if you will have the goodness to accept from me the sum of . . .

He whispers into the First Philanthropist's ear. She is astounded.

First Philanthropist   Mr Scrooge!

The Second Philanthropist indicates she wishes to be told. The First whispers to the Second the amount. The Second Philanthropist is also astounded.

Second Philanthropist   Mr Scrooge!

First Philanthropist   Lord bless us, Mr Scrooge, are you
                 serious?

Scrooge   Not a penny less. I have, since our meeting,
                 walked through the streets you spoke of and a
                 great many back payments are included in that
                 sum, I assure you. Will you come and see me?

First Philanthropist   My dear Sir, we will. I don't know what to
                 say.

Scrooge   Say nothing. Come and see me.

They shake hands.

First Philanthropist   We will.

Scrooge   I am much obliged. Thank you fifty times.

*Scrooge takes out the invitation again and gives it
another straightening. He exits laughing. We hear
jolly party music mixed with the sound of laughter.
Florence enters, laughing. Tupper enters in a
blindfold, pursuing Florence.*

Florence   Tupper, stop it. Please. The others.

From offstage.

Party guest   Tupper, what are you doing, Sir?

Tupper   Nothing. Playing Blind Man's Buff.

*Ebenezer Scrooge enters in a new coat. He is not
seen. Florence is quiet as Tupper chases her. At
last, she slips round him and exits as a peal of
laughter comes from the next room. At this
moment, Scrooge makes a move which Tupper
hears. Tupper moves to Scrooge thinking it is
Florence. He stalks Scrooge.*

And now. Who can this be?

*He then catches up with Scrooge who has been
enjoying the chase.*

Now, my little bird.

Slowly, he starts to feel Scrooge's clothing. He then feels the face.

Ahhhhhh.

He starts to freeze and removes his blindfold.

Help. Help! Fred! It's your Uncle Scrooge and here to murder you.

Scrooge   No. No. My dear Tupper.

The sound of people coming to Tupper's rescue.

Tupper   How do you know my name, Sir?

Scrooge disengages as Fred and the party enter.

Fred   Tupper, who is that with you?

Tupper   Him! Him!

There is a pause and much astonishment.

Scrooge   Fred. I have come to dinner. May I?

Scrooge holds out his invitation. All look amazed.

Fred   Uncle Scrooge. It is. Bless my soul. Is it really you?

He points to his new coat

Scrooge   This?

Rather proud of it.

Oh yes.

Fred leaps forward and picks up Scrooge. Another moves in, so Scrooge is shoulder high. Music strikes up.

Fred   May you come? You, Sir, will do us the honour of leading us into dinner. You have come just in time, Uncle, and your place is set.

Scrooge   Is it, Fred? Is it?

Scrooge weeps. Then he sees Mrs Fred Scrooge whom he has never received. Mrs Fred Scrooge does not come forward. There is a pause as they look at each other. Scrooge puts out his arms with a thousand apologies. She rushes to be embraced.

Mrs Fred   Uncle Scrooge.

Great applause.

Scrooge   You are good souls. All very good souls. And I feel at home already. After all these wasted years.

He starts to perk up.

Well, the years that remain will not be wasted. You will all hold me to that, I know.

They all affirm this loudly in various ways. The music livens into a conga.

Fred   Uncle, lead on.

Scrooge   I beg you join the crocodile for a truly wonderful dinner.

Then quickly to Tupper.

You, Sir, hold this charming girl's waist behind me.

Tupper does so.

Are you comfortable, Tupper?

All laugh.

Tupper   Yes, Sir, Mr Scrooge! And Mr Scrooge, I promised to put ten pounds in your hand if you should come.

Tupper holds out the ten pound note.

Scrooge   Not in my hand, Tupper. Later you and I will go out into the streets and find families who have no dinner, for I fear there are many. What do you say?

Tupper   It will be a pleasure, Mr Scrooge.

Scrooge launches off the conga. He dances outrageously and leads them off stage. The Narrator peels off from the party group.

Scene Seven

Narrator And that was the beginning of the most wonderful day that Scrooge had ever spent. Wonderful party, wonderful games, wonderful happiness.

Scrooge has left the conga and is starting to return to the office which is being set up. He is taking his new coat off and hiding and replacing it with his old shabby and dark coat, so that he is back to his appearance of the earlier scenes.

Now there was one thing Scrooge had to do. He dared not sleep that night for he had to be in at the office very early the next morning. If only he could be there first and catch Bob Cratchit coming late. That was the thing he had set his heart upon.

Scrooge is practising his growl. He laughs.

Scrooge Bah humbug! Hmmmm. Bah humbug! Ah. Hmm. Grrrrrr.

Narrator The clock struck nine. No Bob. A quarter past. No Bob. It was a full eighteen and a half minutes past nine when . . .

Bob Cratchit enters furtively. He tiptoes to his desk and sits. He slowly starts writing, trying not to make a sound. Scrooge looks up from the desk. He doesn't act straight away. Scrooge lets Bob think he has got away with it. Bob's pen squeaks. Scrooge slowly looks up.

Scrooge Hello. What do you mean, Sir, by coming here at this time of day?

Cratchit I am sorry, Sir. I am behind in my time.

Scrooge You are. Yes, I think you are, Sir. Step down, Sir, if you please.

Cratchit It is only once a year, Sir. It shall not be repeated. I was making rather merry yesterday, Sir.

Scrooge Now I'll tell you what, my friend. I'm not going to stand this sort of thing any longer. No, I'm not. No, I am not. And therefore . . .

He jabs Bob.

and therefore, I am going . . . to raise your salary.

There is a long pause. Great shock on Cratchit's face. Scrooge laughs.

Cratchit Aghhhh. Now you just wait there, Mr Scrooge. Don't excite yourself. Hello. Police!

Cratchit has grabbed something to protect himself with.

Scrooge No. No. My dear Bob, not at all. A Merry Christmas. A merrier Christmas, my good fellow, than I've given you for many a long year. I'll raise your salary and endeavour to assist your struggling family and we will discuss your affairs over a Christmas bowl of Smoking Bishop before you dot another 'i', Bob Cratchit! Can you recommend a good Inn, Bob? Not a cheap one, Bob. A comfortable one.

After another shocked pause.

Cratchit An Inn, Sir? I can, Sir. Oh yes, I think I can.

Scrooge Then leave your pen, Sir. Work on Boxing Day? Never again. What do you say, Bob?

Cratchit Never again, Sir.

Scrooge Never again, Sir. Come.

Cratchit	After you, Mr Scrooge.
Scrooge	By no means. By no means. After you, Mr Cratchit.

They bow to each other. Scrooge returns and looks to the heavens.

Spirits, Jacob, if you are watching me, thank you. And inform Mr Fezziwig that he will live again in me. You have my word, Spirits, you have my word.

And with a smile Scrooge steps to one side. The company has entered.

Narrator	And Scrooge was better than his word. He did it all and infinitely more. And to Tiny Tim who did not die, he was a second father.

Tiny Tim joins Scrooge and is raised as the Narrator continues.

He became as good a man as the good old City knew. And it was always said of him that he knew how to keep Christmas if any man alive possessed the knowledge. May that be truly said of us. And so, as Tiny Tim observed . . .

Tiny Tim	God bless us every one.
All	God bless us every one.
Carollers	Now Christmas is over and the wassail begins, Pray open your doors and let us come in, With our wassail. Wassail. Wassail. And joy come to our jolly wassail. Now all you kind people who live far and near, We wish you a Merry Christmas and a Happy New Year. With our wassail. Wassail. Wassail. And joy come to our jolly wassail.

We wish you a Merry Christmas,
We wish you a Merry Christmas,
We wish you a Merry Christmas.
And a Happy New year.
Good tidings we bring – to you and your King,
We wish you a Merry Christmas,
And a Happy New Year.

The End.

QUESTIONS AND EXPLORATIONS

1 Keeping Track

Act One: Scene One

1 What purpose do the Carollers serve in the first scene?

2 How does the playwright create a picture of Victorian England?

3 What are your first impressions of Ebenezer Scrooge and Bob Cratchit?

4 Why does Bob Cratchit want to leave work early?

5 Why was Scrooge not part of the Carolling group?

6 What is Scrooge's attitude towards:

- Bob Cratchit
- his nephew, Fred
- the Carollers
- the two philanthropists?

In what ways is his behaviour to each of them similar and in what ways is it different?

7 What is Fred Scrooge like? How do we know this?

Act One: Scene Two

1 Who is Jacob Marley?
When he appears why is he dressed the way he is?

2 What does Scrooge think is happening?

3 Why does Jacob Marley walk in heavy chains?

4 What does Jacob Marley say will happen to Scrooge?

Act One: Scene Three

1   Where does the Ghost of Christmas Past take Scrooge first? How do they get there? What do they see together?

2   Why does Scrooge weep when he sees the Young Scrooge?

3   What are your impressions of Mr and Mrs Fezziwig?

4   In the scene between Teenage Scrooge and Belle why does the adult Scrooge scream 'No. Mercy good spirit'?

5   Why is it important that we see Belle happily married with Charlie? How would Scrooge feel?

6   What is the tone of this scene? How does Scrooge feel as he is shown the various shadows of things that have been?

Act One: Scene Four

1   What is Scrooge's attitude to the Ghost of Christmas Present?

2   Why do you think the playwright brings the Carollers on stage at the end of this scene?

Act Two: Scene One

1   What is Christmas like in the Cratchit household?

2   How do the Cratchits show their sense of fun in this scene?

3   Why do we have sympathy for Tiny Tim?

4   What does Scrooge fear to see in the future for the Cratchits?

5   In what way are the Cratchits 'poor but very rich' as the Ghost of Christmas Present says?

6   What are Mrs Cratchit's feelings about Scrooge?

Act Two: Scene Two

1   Why does the Ghost of Christmas Present show Scrooge the sights in this scene?

Act Two: Scene Three

1   What is the party at Fred Scrooge's house like? How is it different from Christmas Day at the Cratchits?

2   What does Tupper want in this scene when playing Blind Man's Buff? How does he cheat?

3   How do you think Scrooge feels when he discovers what Fred was really thinking of during the game of 'Yes and No'?

Act Two: Scene Four

1   Why do you think the Ghost of Christmas Present takes Scrooge on his travels across the world?

2   What is the purpose of the carols in this scene?

3   Who are Ignorance and Need? Why does Scrooge not want to see them?

Act Two: Scene Five

1   How is the Ghost of Christmas Future different from the other spirits?

2   Where does the Ghost of Christmas Future take Scrooge?

3   Who is Old Scratch?

4   What does Scrooge discover at the end of the scene? How does he feel?

Act Two: Scene Six

1 When Scrooge wakes up how does he feel?

2 What actions does Scrooge immediately take when he realises that he is still alive?

3 How is this scene similar to the opening scene of the play and how is it very different?

4 Why would Tupper be surprised that Scrooge knows his name?

Act Two: Scene Seven

1 In what ways will Mr Fezziwig live again in Scrooge?

2 What has Scrooge learned?

2   Explorations

A   Characters

1 Why is there a narrator in the play? What does the narrator do that the characters in the play could not do?

2 Describe how Scrooge changes from the beginning of the play to the end of the play. Find a line from the beginning and a line from the end which show this change in his character.

3 Choose three important moments in the play which you think help to make Scrooge become a better person.

4 What do you think Scrooge should look like? How should he move and what should he sound like?

5 Mrs Cratchit thinks that Scrooge treats Bob Cratchit badly. Do you agree? If so, list the ways in which Scrooge is mean to Cratchit.

6 Why does Cratchit keep working for Scrooge?
In pairs, one of you role play Cratchit and the other role play Mrs Cratchit. Mrs Cratchit is trying to persuade her husband to stop working for Scrooge, but he wants to stay.

7 Cratchit and Tiny Tim are very close. Talk about their relationship and work out what makes it special.

8 Why does Fred always lay a place for his Uncle Scrooge at table?

9 Explain why you think Belle breaks her engagement to Scrooge. What do you think she would be like now if she had stayed with Scrooge?

10 List three differences in the way Mr Fezziwig treats Ebenezer and Dick and the way Scrooge treats Cratchit.

11 In some productions of this play, all the actors (except for the one playing Scrooge) might have to play many parts. There is not much time in between scenes for the actors to change their costumes, so we have to find other ways of telling the audience about the characters that they are playing.
Choose either one item of clothing, or one object for each character, that the actor can use to tell the audience who they are and what they are like.

12 Why does Jacob Marley come back and help Scrooge?

13 Look at the three ghosts who come to visit Scrooge. Talk about how they show Scrooge different things and what the main differences are between them.

B Further Activities

1 The playwright has not described what the ghosts should look like. Choose one of them and design a costume for it, thinking about what it says and does, how it should move and speak.

2   The ghosts show Scrooge things he has done that he is not
    proud of.
    Work in groups. Each of you should take turns in being the
    director.

    a) Think of something you have done that you are not proud
       of.
    b) Set up your scene as you remember it, telling the actors
       what they should say and do.
    c) Watch the scene in the way that Scrooge has to watch
       scenes from his past.
    d) Set up the scene again but this time change it so you are
       proud of the way you behaved.

3   Work in pairs. One person role play Old Scrooge and one
    person role play the Young Scrooge. The Old Scrooge has to
    try and persuade the Young Scrooge to act more sensibly, not
    to lose Belle and to be more caring towards Fred.

4   List the ways in which Scrooge shows he is greedy.
    List the ways in which you are greedy.
    Then list the ways in which you think you are or could be
    generous.

5   Suggest a setting that could work for the whole play. Think
    about: all the different locations in the play; what each scene
    needs – furniture, lighting, props, etc; what time the play is set
    in.

6   Play the 'Yes or No' game, which the guests play at Fred's
    party. The characters or places or objects must all be referred
    to in the play.

GLOSSARY

14	*hearse*	carriage used for the transport of coffins
15	*condemned*	forced to do something
19	*pitch-black*	with no light at all
20	*reclamation*	return to a better way of life
25	*shove-ha'penny*	a table game using coins
25	*dandies*	smart men
25	*philosophers*	thinkers
26	*skinflint*	mean person
27	*buffet*	light meal
28	*fiancée*	girl who is engaged to be married
29	*sovereign*	old British money, worth £1.00
33	*sweet meats*	sweets normally containing sugar, chocolate or fruit
35	*parade*	public procession
35	*dismay*	worry
37	*lame*	unable to walk
38	*regiment*	a large group of soldiers
39	*vacant*	empty
39	*surplus*	what remains over, the excess
40	*odious*	hateful
40	*stingy*	mean
41	*harrow*	plough
44	*claw*	a hand, here like that of a bird or skeleton
45	*jackanapes*	lively person
45	*wag*	a joker, a funny person
47	*duck-billed platypus*	Australian web-footed animal
48	*wombat*	Australian mammal, like a furry pig

49	*score*	reason
52	*spectre*	a ghost
52	*waning*	fading, in the sense of time running out
52	*The Stock Exchange*	the place in the City of London where dealers in stocks and shares work
53	*snuff*	powdered tobacco taken by sniffing up nostrils
54	*Rag-a-bone!*	the call of someone dealing in old clothes
54	*merchandise*	goods
54	*purloin*	steal
55	*face*	cheek
54	*grim reaper*	death personified as a stern old man who cuts people down like corn
57	*In memoriam*	Latin for 'in memory of'
59	*reign*	a King or Queen's time on the throne
60	*poulterers*	sellers of ducks, geese, chickens and turkeys
61	*errand*	simple job, usually for small payment